RAF BOMBER CREWMAN

Jonathan Falconer

SHIRE PUBLICATIONS

Published in Great Britain in 2010 by Shire Publications Ltd, Midland House, West Way, Botley, Oxford OX2 0PH, United Kingdom.

44-02 23rd Street, Suite 219, Long Island City, NY 11101, USA.

E-mail: shire@shirebooks.co.uk www.shirebooks.co.uk

A CIP catalogue record for this book is available from the British Library.

Shire Library no. 602. ISBN-13: 978 0 74780 796 4

Designed by Tony Truscott Designs, Sussex, UK and typeset in Perpetua and Gill Sans.

Printed in China through Worldprint Ltd.

10 11 12 13 14 10 9 8 7 6 5 4 3 2 1

COVER IMAGE

Mildenhall, Suffolk, 16 January 1942. The crew of a 149 Squadron Short Stirling pose for the camera as their aircraft is bombed-up. (IWM TR135)

TITLE PAGE IMAGE

Souvenir programme for *Target for Tonight*, the wartime film about RAF Bomber Command, featuring the crew of Wellington bomber 'F' for Freddie.

CONTENTS PAGE IMAGE

The pilot of an RAF aircraft was always the captain, regardless of his rank, and once in the air his word was law. This pilot of a Handley Page Halifax of 35 Squadron is preparing to take off from RAF Linton-on-Ouse, Yorkshire, in 1941. (IWM D6051)

DEDICATION

To my cousin, Flight Sergeant Leslie Fry, RAFVR, Flight Engineer, 429 Squadron, RCAF, killed in action over Holland, 30 November 1944.

ACKNOWLEDGEMENTS

I should like to thank the following people and institutions who have allowed me to use illustrations, which are acknowledged as follows:

Jarrod Cotter, page 39 (top); Imperial War Museum, pages 3, 6 (both), 7 (top), 8, 10 (top), 11 (top right), 14 (top), 15 (bottom), 19 (bottom), 20 (bottom), 24 (both), 26 (top), 27 (both), 29 (top), 31 (both), 32, 34 (both), 35, 38 (top), 40 (both), 42, 43 (both), 46 (bottom right), 47 (bottom), 48 (top), 49 (both), 54, 55, 56, 57, 58 and 62; Public Archives of Canada, pages 26 (bottom) and 44; RAF Museum, page 39 (bottom). Patrick and Deb Falconer for kindly allowing me to photograph the items of flying kit that appear on pages 51–3. All other illustrations are from the author's collection.

CONTENTS

"Bristol" WRITES WORLD HISTORY
AIR MINISTRY COMMUNIQUE.
A POWERFUL FORCE OF OUR HEAVY BOMBERS WAS OUT OVER GERMANY LAST NIGHT. LARGE BOMB LOADS WERE CARRIED BY OUR STIRLINGS, THE MOST POWERFUL BOMBERS IN THE WORLD.
"Bristol" HERCULES ENGINES

PROLOGUE: THE SIX-YEAR OFFENSIVE

THE FOCUS of this book is on the RAF's heavy night bomber crews of the Second World War. Barely out of their teens, they were the men who flew the Short Stirling, Handley Page Halifax and Avro Lancaster heavy bombers into battle. 'Bomber' Harris's 'old lags' – as they were endearingly known to their tough commander-in-chief – were at the tip of a spear behind which lay RAF Bomber Command's huge infrastructure of airfields, groundcrews, administrative staff, cooks, drivers and armourers. Their sole purpose was to launch skywards each night these heavy bomber crews and their aircraft to strike at the centres of population and industry inside Nazi Germany.

Within hours of the declaration of war on 3 September 1939, an RAF Bristol Blenheim bomber took off and headed towards the north German port of Wilhelmshaven to photograph Nazi warships. In so doing it became the first RAF aircraft of the war to cross the German frontier. In the devastating world war that followed, Bomber Command played a crucial part in toppling Hitler's so-called 'thousand-year Reich'.

In the first year of war the RAF's ill-prepared bomber crews learned some hard lessons after enemy defences decimated their squadrons on daylight raids. Such unsustainable losses of men and machines quickly forced the high commanders to rethink their strategy. They realised that if Bomber Command wanted to avoid heavy casualties, the only way to pursue an effective bombing campaign was under the cover of darkness.

Air Chief Marshal Sir Arthur 'Bomber' Harris, who took control of Bomber Command in 1942, believed that bombing held the key to the defeat of Nazi Germany. Strategic bombing on a large enough scale, relentlessly pressed home, would lead to the collapse of German industry and the morale of its population. In a massive and sustained offensive, the industrial cities of the German Reich were pounded by Harris's bombers almost nightly until the end of the war, causing huge material damage and heavy loss of civilian life.

Britain's daily papers and BBC Home Service's newsreaders became regular narrators of the RAF's bomber offensive, with reports of how 'last

Opposite: An advertisement for the Bristol Hercules engines that powered the RAF's Short Stirling heavy bomber. These dependable radial engines were also used in certain marks of the RAF's Vickers Wellington, Handley Page Halifax and Avro Lancaster bombers.

The Handley Page Hampden medium bomber was known as the flying panhandle because of its slender fuselage. This 83 Squadron crew are pictured during the invasion summer of 1940. (IWM CH256)

night our bombers raided targets in the Ruhr valley again'. The RAF and its bomber crews became the darlings of the news media, an enviable position they occupied for much of the war.

While the heavies hit Germany by night, the medium bomber squadrons of Bomber Command's 2 Group continued to mount daring but often costly daylight raids against enemy targets in occupied Europe and in Germany itself. Later in the war, de Havilland Mosquitoes of the Command's Light Night Striking Force waged an effective campaign against Berlin and other targets.

By far the greatest damage upon Germany was inflicted in the final six months of war, at which point Bomber Command was able to strike massive and highly destructive blows against area and precision targets. But the cost to Bomber Command was massive: over 6,000 aircraft were lost and more than 47,000 aircrew killed or missing.

The chapters that follow describe how Britain and its Empire mobilised its manpower resources to help supply Bomber Command with crews, how

In 1939 the Vickers Wellington was the RAF's most effective bomber aircraft and formed the backbone of the early offensive. Here, crews from 149 Squadron pose with a Wellington after their return from the first bombing raid on Berlin, 25/26 August 1940. (IWM HU44271)

The superlative Avro Lancaster was arguably the best bomber of the war, on either side. As the sun sets, Lancs of 57 Squadron wait on their dispersals at RAF Scampton, Lincolnshire, before an operation in February 1943. (IWM CH8785)

these men were trained and what they did once they joined a frontline bomber squadron. Also covered is the specialist flying clothing that was developed to help crewmen cope with the extremes of temperature and altitude. Miraculously, many RAF bomber crewmen survived what was one of the most dangerous occupations of the Second World War – a job eclipsed only in its scale of losses by the Japanese Kamikazes and the German U-boat service.

The war years spawned dozens of publications, both official and commercial, that told of Bomber Command's exploits to an eager public. Here are three such titles, published in 1941 and 1942.

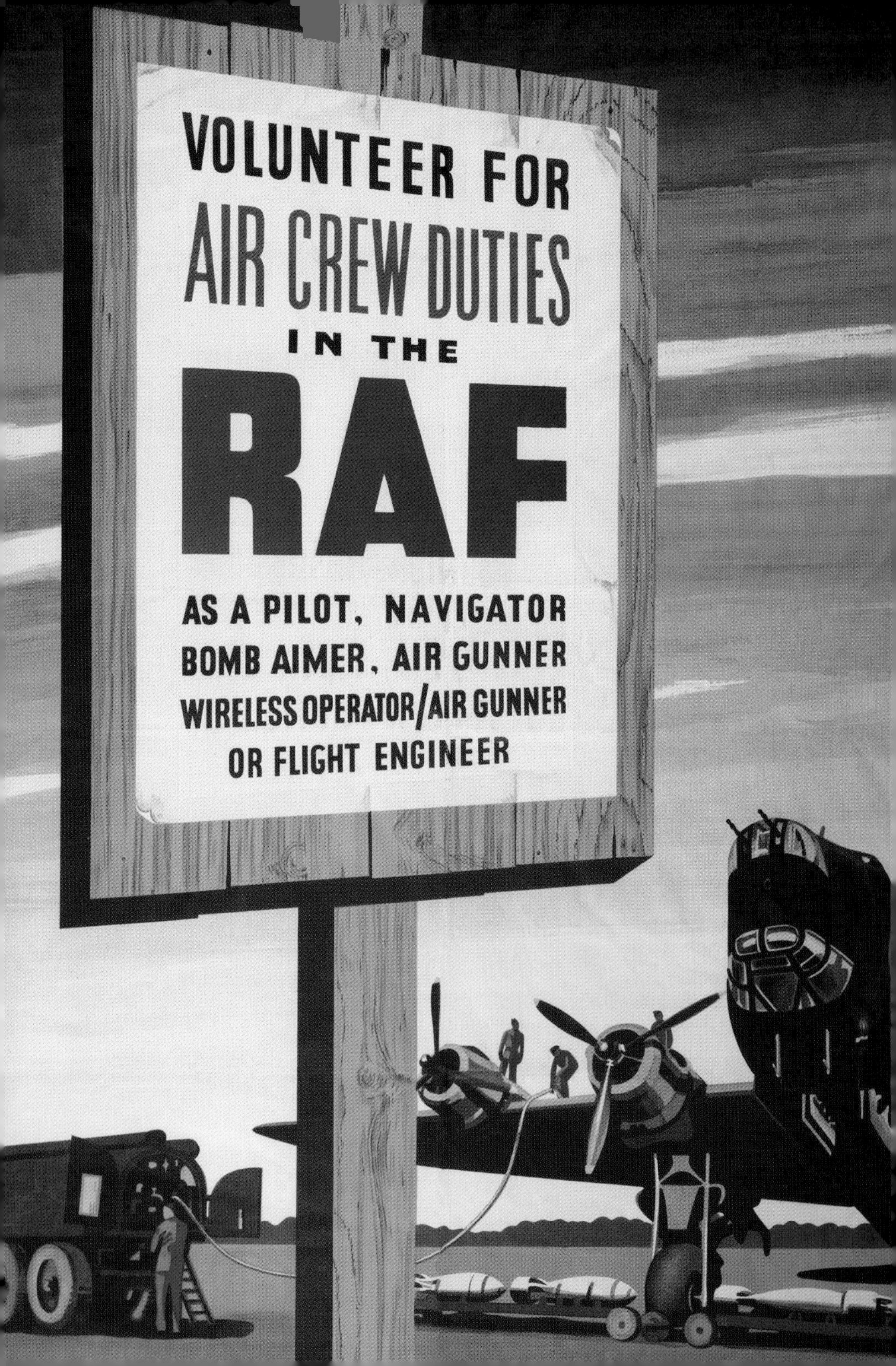

VOLUNTEER FOR
AIR CREW DUTIES
IN THE
RAF

AS A PILOT, NAVIGATOR
BOMB AIMER, AIR GUNNER
WIRELESS OPERATOR/AIR GUNNER
OR FLIGHT ENGINEER

WHO WERE THE 'BOMBER BOYS'?

Bomber Command and its crews were probably unique in the history of warfare. The Command itself was a truly cosmopolitan affair, attracting men from the far corners of the Empire and from the Nazi-occupied countries of Europe and Scandinavia. A typical RAF bomber crew was a microcosm of Bomber Command itself, reflecting this broad international mix. By January 1945 the manpower contribution from the Empire had risen, with nearly half of Bomber Command's pilots coming from Canada, Australia or New Zealand.

All RAF bomber aircrew were volunteers, and in the case of the specialist target markers of 8 Group – the Pathfinder Force – many were volunteers within a volunteer force. Canada was unique among the Dominions in contributing a complete bomber group, No. 6, while other countries contributed entire squadrons. Towards the end of the war most bomber crews were made up of volunteers (RAFVR) who, at the beginning of the war, had still been schoolboys. Those who had been regulars in the pre-war RAF and who had survived the culling of six years of war, were by now in a distinct minority.

At the outbreak of war the crew of a typical twin-engined light bomber like the Bristol Blenheim comprised a pilot, an observer/bomb-aimer and a wireless operator/air gunner. By the war's end the crew of a four-engined heavy bomber like the Avro Lancaster could number up to eight men: pilot, navigator, flight engineer, bomb-aimer, wireless operator, mid-upper gunner, tail gunner and perhaps an extra gunner, navigator or 'special operator'.

As the war gathered momentum the growing size and complexity of bomber aircraft made it necessary for the RAF to think again about the composition of its bomber crews, bringing in new and specialised crew trades while revising the duties of existing ones.

Since the earliest days of the RAF, when it became clear that more than one person was needed to crew a large aircraft, the most important figure in any aircrew had always been the pilot. In most cases he was a commissioned officer (although many bomber pilots in the Second World

Opposite: An RAF recruiting poster from about 1941. The British news media painted a glamorous picture of life as a flyer, so there was never a shortage of willing applicants. (IWM PST3726)

Fresh-faced recruits march off to collect their kit at the RAF Aircrew Reception Centre in London's Regent's Park in 1942. (IWM CH10988)

War were NCOs) and was designated the captain of the aircraft. Along with two other key crewmembers, the navigator and the bomb-aimer, the leadership qualities of these three men were vital to the cohesion of a Second World War RAF bomber crew. Leadership – or displaying 'officer-like qualities' – reflected strongly the public-school ethos of the period.

Initially, more pilots, navigators and bomb-aimers became commissioned officers on completion of their flying training than the other aircrew categories – the so-called 'tradesmen' like air gunners, wireless operators and flight engineers. Of those who were commissioned out of the former group, many were likely to have been educated at public school. More than a few who were not from this background suspected that the 'old school tie' network lay behind commissioning policy. But the need for aircrew continued to grow as the bomber offensive gained momentum and the original supply of public-school candidates began to dwindle, forcing the RAF to open its aircrew ranks to a wider social catchment. Soon, it was the turn of men who were products of the grammar and county schools to swell the ranks of the RAF's bomber crews.

Pre-war 'regular' Squadron Leader David Drakes (second from front) and his 49 Squadron Hampden crew went missing on 1 November 1941. By the late-war period few experienced 'regulars' were left alive and had been replaced largely by volunteers who were still at school when the war began.

Far left:
This newspaper advertisement from 1941 makes an appeal for trainee bomber pilots. The elite status of the job is shamelessly extolled – 'a job that calls for fitness, dash, initiative, intelligence, responsibility'.

Left: Sergeant Lincoln Orville Lynch from Jamaica trained as an air gunner in 1942. On his first operational flight with 102 Squadron he shot down a German night fighter. Lynch was later awarded the Distinguished Flying Medal. (IWM CH12263)

Aircrew basic training was undertaken at one of the many Initial Training Wings (ITW) scattered across England. Successful graduates were then shipped overseas for flying training on Tiger Moth and North American Harvard aircraft at Service Flying Training Schools (SFTS) many thousands of miles away in the safety of the Dominions and the USA under the aegis of the British Commonwealth Air Training Plan (BCATP). Flight engineers were trained in the UK.

Flying Training Command produced qualified pilots, navigators, bomb-aimers, wireless operators and air gunners, and passed them on to Bomber Command via Operational Training Units, which turned them into combat-ready aircrews. Crews destined for the Mosquito bomber squadrons underwent separate operational training at the Mosquito Training Unit in the Pathfinder Force.

The pilot, whether he was an officer or an NCO, was always the captain of the aircraft. All decisions ultimately rested with him. He was identified by the flying brevet with two wings either side of a laurel wreath surrounding the letters RAF, surmounted by a king's crown, above his left breast pocket. The

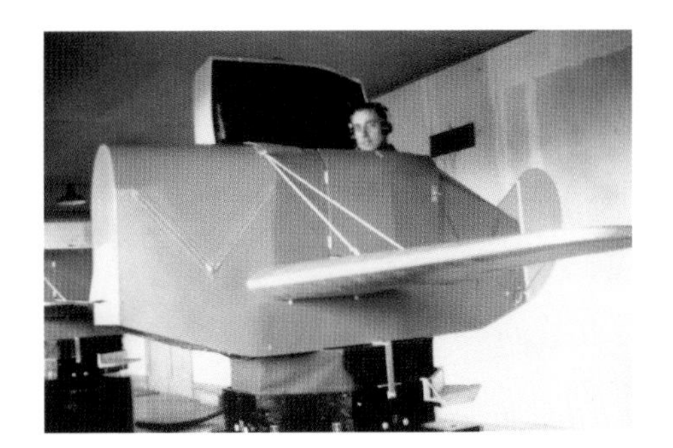

The American-designed Link Trainer was the 1940s equivalent of a modern aircraft flight simulator. It was a key pilot training aid that was used by almost every combatant nation during the Second World War, including the RAF, as a safe way to teach new pilots how to fly by instruments.

Right: Airmen training for duties in the RAF could be identified by the white flash in the front of their side caps. These were worn until training was complete, when they received their 'wings'.

Menu

Assorted Salted Nuts — Casaba Melon

Seafood Cocktail

Cream of Mushrooms au Crout

Grilled Tenderloin Steak

New Peas in Mint — Potatoes Chateau

Blackstone Salad

Rainbow Parfait, Petit Four

Rolls and Butter

Coffee — Tea

Far right: More RAF bomber crews were trained in Canada than anywhere else. This menu is from the end-of-course dinner for 31 Elementary Flying Training School at Calgary.

same design applied to pilots from Canada, Australia and New Zealand, but with the letters replaced by RCAF, RAAF or RNZAF respectively.

With the move to night operations in 1940, bomber aircraft began flying ever increasing distances and it became clear that a navigation specialist was required. Although the aircrew category of observer (designated by the flying 'O' half-wing brevet, but without the laurel wreath), which had been around since the First World War and who performed the duty of second aircrewmember responsible for navigation, bomb-aiming and any other task called upon to do by the pilot, it was clearly insufficient because the pilot was still the primary navigator. Not until the introduction of the specialist navigator category in 1942, identified by the 'N' half-wing brevet, did the situation change. Now that the roles of pilot and navigator had been more clearly defined, a requirement for further specialist categories became apparent – that of the air bomber ('B') and flight engineer ('E').

A greater variety of bombs were now in use by the RAF and with them came more complex bombsights (for aiming them) and bomb-release mechanisms (for

Below: In 1943, there were 153 Flying Training Schools in the UK, 92 in Canada, 26 in Australia, 25 in South Africa, 10 in South Rhodesia, 9 in India, 6 each in New Zealand and the Middle East, one in the Bahamas and 5 in the USA.

dropping the load). Analysis of early raids had identified the need for two specialists in a bomber crew: the navigator to take the bomber to the target area, and an air bomber to take over from him to make the final run-in to the target where he would aim and release the bombs. Along with the flight engineer category, that of the air bomber was introduced at about the same time as the navigator.

The advent of the four-engined bomber, of which the first in the RAF was the Short Stirling, led to the creation of the flight engineer trade to handle the complicated mechanical, hydraulic, electrical and fuel systems during flight. He also acted as a link with the groundcrew that serviced the bomber. The first officially trained flight engineers began arriving on the squadrons in April 1941, although it was not until September 1942 that official recognition was forthcoming with the introduction of the specialist 'E' flying brevet. Up until the autumn of 1944, flight engineers for Canadian heavy bomber squadrons in England were in short supply because the RCAF did not train aircrew in this trade.

Defence of the bomber against enemy fighters lay in the hands of the air gunner. Before the war he was a ground staff armament tradesman who could be called upon as the need arose to fly as an air gunner, for which he was paid only for the time he spent in the air. He wore a brass-winged bullet on each sleeve, but for him flying was a secondary duty. Not until May 1940 did the Air Ministry officially decree that all aircrew tradesmen (that is, air gunners and wireless operator/air gunners) should be promoted from the ranks to the minimum rank of sergeant. This promotion applied to all other ranks who had completed training in their aircrew trade category and who were flying operationally. There were two aircrew trades that came under the air gunner category: wireless operator/air gunner and air gunner. Both were identified by the twelve-feather half-wing brevet with a laurel wreath surrounding the letters 'AG'. Wireless operators were identified by the addition of 'sparks' badges on each sleeve above their rank stripes, although a few 'WAG' brevets were issued.

From mid-1943 the importance to Bomber Command of the new 'black arts' of radar and radio countermeasures became increasingly plain. On the main force squadrons it was not uncommon for an extra (eighth) crewmember to be carried to operate the H2S set (ground mapping radar). He was usually a navigator and was known as the 'Y' operator, 'Y' equipment being another code name for the H2S.

A new aircrew category was added to a handful of 'special duty' bomber squadrons in the newly designated 100 (Bomber Support) Group. This was known as 'special operator', or 'spec op' for short, and the job entailed operating on-board electronic jamming equipment that was able to disrupt

RAF aircrew flying brevets were badges of qualification that were worn on uniform tunics and battledress blouses. From top to bottom: pilot, observer, navigator, bomb-aimer, air gunner, flight engineer, wireless operator/air gunner.

Sergeant 'Dusty' Miller, the mid-upper gunner of a 57 Squadron Lancaster, scans the sky from inside the Perspex cupola of his Frazer-Nash power-operated turret. The protuberance beneath the twin Browning .303 machine guns is part of the 'taboo track' device that stopped mid-upper gunners from shooting the tails off their own aircraft.
(IWM CH8795)

ONE AIRMAN'S WAR: GROUP CAPTAIN HAMISH MAHADDIE DSO, DFC, AFC, CZMC (1911–97)

In February 1943, Wing Commander Hamish Mahaddie received the DSO, DFC, AFC and Czech Military Cross in the same ceremony at Buckingham Palace – surely an RAF record. A short, stocky Scot from Edinburgh, Mahaddie joined the RAF as part of the 17th Entry at Halton in 1928. He trained as a pilot in the Middle East and gained his wings in 1935. During the Second World War he completed two tours of operations as a bomber pilot, the first with 77 Squadron flying Whitleys, and the second with 7 Squadron on Stirlings, before joining the headquarters staff of the Pathfinder Force. His job as 'horse thief' to the Pathfinder commander Air Commodore Donald Bennett, was to find, select and train future Pathfinder crews from the main force squadrons. It was his skill in selecting crews that helped make the Pathfinder Force the elite band that it had become by the war's end.

After the war Hamish helped introduce the Canberra bomber into RAF service and upon his retirement in 1958, as a group captain, he acted as a technical adviser to the British film industry. His terrific sense of humour and legendary storytelling skills concealed a deep-rooted commitment to the RAF and a lifelong loyalty to his Pathfinder 'boss' Don Bennett. He died on 16 January 1997, aged eighty-five.

Tour-expired bomber crews were posted to training units to instruct novice crews. These instructors are with 1651 HCU at RAF Waterbeach in 1942.

radio communications between German nightfighter pilots and their ground controllers. Spec ops were selected from all aircrew categories and every man was a German language speaker. Some were German-born, others were German Jews – the latter taking an extra personal risk whenever they flew over enemy territory.

Air gunners under training prepare to fire twin .303 machine guns mounted on a tripod at a firing range in 1942. (IWM COL209)

LIFE ON A BOMBER AIRFIELD

ON COMPLETION of training, a novice RAF heavy bomber crew would be posted to a bomber squadron based at one of the many airfields that dotted the eastern counties of England.

A bomber airfield usually hosted two heavy bomber squadrons. Each squadron averaged twenty aircraft and twenty crews of seven men each, split into three divisions or 'Flights' – A, B and C. The ratio of ground staff to aircrew was about ten to one, giving a population of about 3,000 men and women on a typical wartime bomber airfield.

For bomber crews who were lucky enough to be posted to one of the 'permanent' bomber stations that had been built before the war, their living conditions were comfortable. Officers' quarters on permanent stations were usually in stone-built accommodation wings on each side of the neo-Georgian Mess building. Senior officers had large rooms, each subdivided into a sitting room and a bedroom, while junior officers had just one room. Meals were eaten in the Mess dining room where facilities also included a billiard room and a comfortable anteroom in which to relax and listen to the gramophone or read the daily papers.

The Sergeants' Mess was similarly well appointed. It had a dining room on the ground floor and bedrooms on the first floor, arranged each side of a central corridor, and in two attached wings, with communal bathrooms. Two NCO airmen would share a room, simply furnished with twin beds and a dressing table with drawers.

On the 'hostilities only' bomber stations that had sprung up all over eastern England after 1939, accommodation could be spartan. Ever-present mud seemed to characterise these hastily constructed airfields, which were built on requisitioned farmland. Under the wartime dispersed layout system, for safety reasons the living quarters were located well away from the main technical sites. NCO crews were occasionally billeted in long, low-ceilinged barrack huts with concrete floors, which could sleep several crews on iron-framed beds. A single airfield could have as many as twenty-five such barrack huts, each sleeping up to twenty-four airmen.

Opposite: On a wartime RAF bomber airfield bicycle was a necessity of life, particularly since the newly built airfields had widely dispersed domestic and technical sites. Without the benefit of two wheels it would have taken hours to walk from one site to another.

Right: Individual bomber aircraft had their own dispersal pan situated on the airfield perimeter, with an aircrew of seven (generally) and a dedicated groundcrew staff with a flight sergeant ('chiefy') in charge. This is an Avro Manchester of 83 Squadron with its crew at RAF Scampton in April 1942.

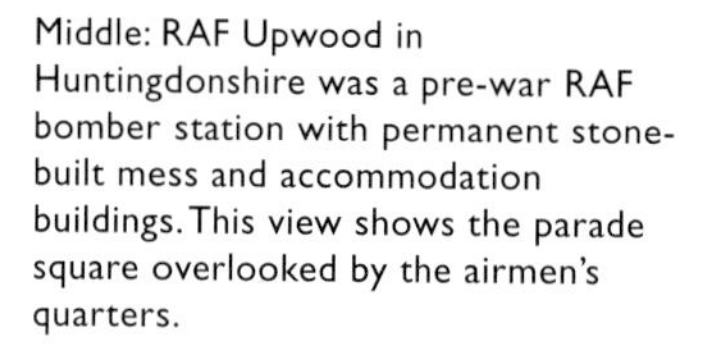

Middle: RAF Upwood in Huntingdonshire was a pre-war RAF bomber station with permanent stone-built mess and accommodation buildings. This view shows the parade square overlooked by the airmen's quarters.

Below: A squadron usually comprised twenty-four aircraft. Individual aircraft, aircrews and groundcrews were allocated to a particular flight – A, B or C – each of which was made up of some eight aircraft and occupied its own assigned corner of the airfield. This is 617 Squadron in July 1943 after the famous dams raid.

This is a dispersed site on the 'hostilities only' RAF bomber airfield at Ludford Magna in Lincolnshire. When one considers the rough and ready appearance of the place it can be easily understood why Ludford's several thousand RAF inhabitants called it 'Mudford Magna'.

Usually, however, an NCO crew would live in a single-room Nissen hut of their own, which was reckoned to be better for morale than the utilitarian barrack block. A junior officer would occupy a single room (one of four). The hut was likely to be located at the edge of an aerodrome, often on the edge of – or even within – woodland, but invariably surrounded by mud.

Because of their young age, most aircrew were unmarried, but a good number were married men. Up until 1942 it was not unusual for an NCO or officer bomber crewman and his wife to live in married quarters on the airfield, or for his wife to 'take rooms' nearby, to where he would repair after a day's or night's duty. Soon after 'Bomber' Harris took over Bomber Command in 1942, he ordered that no wives would be allowed to live within an hour's drive of a bomber airfield. Only those who were already living out were exempted temporarily from this ruling. Britain was engaged in total war and Harris believed that his crews should not be distracted by women and sentiment from the serious business of fighting the enemy.

The Sergeants' or Officers' Mess was usually housed in a prefabricated Nissen hut. It was usually some distance away from the domestic site, which meant a long walk across muddy ground or a short cycle ride. Inside the Mess there were armchairs and magazines, and sometimes a piano. A cylindrical coke stove warmed the room, or if they were lucky a brick hearth with a blazing log fire. With its simple creature comforts the Mess was the closest place to home that a bomber crew would find on a wartime RAF airfield.

A Lancaster crew from 44 Squadron warm themselves around the coke stove inside their Nissen hut at RAF Dunholme Lodge after returning from a raid on Stuttgart, 2 March 1944. (IWM CH12379)

All lino and Utility furniture, this is the scene inside the Sergeants' Mess at RAF Lakenheath in Suffolk. It may look basic, but it was comparatively luxurious when compared to crews' spartan Nissen hut quarters.

As already mentioned, aircrew meals were eaten in the Mess dining rooms where the quality of the food depended on who had sourced and cooked it – no different really to a civilian restaurant. The Mess kitchens were still subject to the same strictures of wartime food rationing as those in Civvy Street, but occasionally when a professionally trained chef was called up into the RAF to serve his country, he might end up on a bomber airfield in the wilds of Lincolnshire. He could work wonders with the simplest ingredients and it did not necessarily follow that he would be cooking for the Officers' Mess, either. Owing to their rural location, some bomber airfield Mess kitchens enjoyed welcome supplements to the meat ration in the form of locally bagged wild rabbit and pheasant.

Tired aircrew eat breakfast in the Sergeants' Mess at RAF Scampton on their return from a raid. These three from 57 Squadron died a month later when their Lancaster crashed returning from Berlin in the early hours of 2 March 1943. (IWM CH8806)

Bomber crews enjoyed a favoured status in the Mess dining rooms over their non-aircrew contemporaries. The simple enquiry, 'Are you flying tonight, Sir?' if answered in the affirmative, meant that a crewman would be served with an 'operational egg' for his flying supper. Food rationing meant that fresh eggs were virtually unavailable to the public at large, so this was a real treat and a privilege.

Crews that had flown on 'ops' the previous night would usually sleep in until about 11 a.m. After lunch in the Mess they

On stand-down nights bomber crews headed for the local pubs and 'flesh pots', or stayed on the airfield for a beer-up in the Mess. This is a scene inside the Sergeants' Mess at RAF Downham Market as Stirling crews of 218 Squadron live for the moment and enjoy a sing-song and a beer.

would report into 'flights' (their respective Flight office) at about 2 p.m. If they were lucky and ops were not planned for the coming night, then they would have a free evening. If they were on again, then it was a repeat of the previous night's routine.

With no ops the crew were stood down and would probably go out for a night on the town, if one was nearby. The larger cities of York, Lincoln and Cambridge were popular with crews, but many found a good night out in the less salubrious surroundings of Doncaster, Grimsby and Hull. Many bomber crews were based at airfields miles away from anywhere, although there was usually a local pub to which they could walk or cycle. Beer was rationed, but landlords would often look kindly on the crews as they knew where they had come from.

Some crews chose to stay on the airfield, sitting at the Mess bar discussing the previous night's flying over a drink. There might be someone who could play the Mess piano and men would stand around singing the popular songs of the day. After four or five hours of drinking and singing they would retire to bed.

Whatever their particular choice of unwinding, bomber crews would have found the experience a little unreal when compared with their previous night of ops. The contrast between the fire and fury of bombing Berlin, say, followed twenty-four hours later by drinking beer and rubbing shoulders with civilians at the bar of an English country pub, enjoying a high tea at Betty's Bar in York, or fun and games at a Mess party when spirits ran high and beer flowed freely, could not have been more stark.

A DAY IN THE LIFE

MODERN WARFARE is often said to be 99 per cent boredom and 1 per cent sheer terror, which is a description that could well be applied to the life of an RAF bomber crewman in the Second World War.

When compared to an infantryman on the battlefield or a sailor on board ship, the bomber crewman's life was very different. Whereas the soldier or sailor might be on campaign or at sea for long periods of time without home leave and creature comforts, the airman was invariably based in Britain and could regularly enjoy clean bed sheets, bacon-and-egg breakfasts and visits to the cinema. On the face of it he appeared to be very lucky, but the reality was rather different.

An RAF bomber crewman inhabited a world of extremes. One night he might be flying in a Lancaster over a burning German city, enduring sub-zero temperatures and living in fear of a well-aimed burst of cannon fire from a German night fighter, or a direct hit from flak. If he survived, the next evening he might be out on the town with his crew for a beer-up, or even taking a romantic cycle ride in the countryside with a 'popsy'. The odds against survival were stacked against him: there was a one-in-four chance he would not even reach four ops before he was killed.

On average a heavy bomber crew might be expected to fly two or three ops in a week, but generally this depended on the time of the year and the weather, the particular phase of the moon and of course operational requirements.

During the Battle of Berlin in the winter months of 1943–44, RAF bomber crews could be flying deep penetration raids on three or more nights in succession to the German capital, in the most adverse weather conditions and at a time when the enemy's defences were at their most deadly. Aircrew losses became critical.

What follows is a typical day and night in the life of an RAF heavy bomber crew during 1943, for participation in a 'Goodwood' – or maximum effort – raid to a target 'somewhere in Germany'.

After breakfast, aircrew report to their flight offices and are told whether operations are planned for the coming night or if there will be a stand-down.

Opposite: The pilot and second pilot of a Short Stirling, framed in the bulkhead doorway that leads through from the flight deck to the flight engineer's compartment. On the right can be seen the engineer's array of dials and switches.

When snow fell across eastern England it was a case of all hands to the brooms and shovels to clear aircraft, taxiways and runways of the white stuff. If a maximum effort was planned, then everyone from the station commander down got stuck in to make sure the resident squadrons could take off. (IWM CH12431)

From the moment that details of the target come through on the telephone from the bomber group headquarters, to the point some eighteen hours later when the last few aircraft land back at their home base, activity on a heavy bomber station is intense to get its squadrons airborne.

Meanwhile, in station headquarters the group broadcast has come through on the telephone requiring a 'Goodwood' (maximum effort) and details of the target for tonight. The bomb load and H-Hour (take-off time) along with route details will follow shortly, but first of all the station intelligence officer notifies everyone who needs to know, from the station, squadron and flight commanders, through to flying control and the bomb dump.

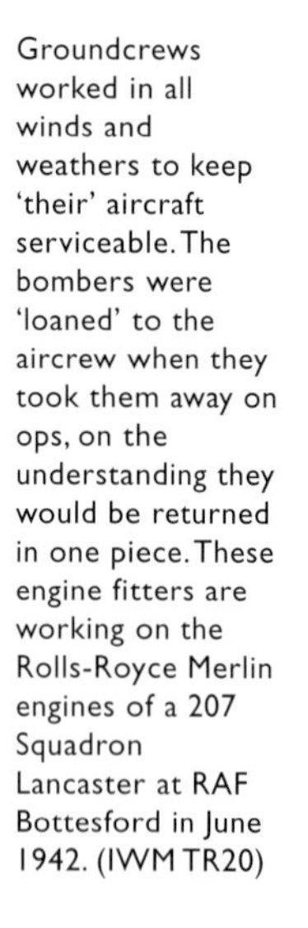

Groundcrews worked in all winds and weathers to keep 'their' aircraft serviceable. The bombers were 'loaned' to the aircrew when they took them away on ops, on the understanding they would be returned in one piece. These engine fitters are working on the Rolls-Royce Merlin engines of a 207 Squadron Lancaster at RAF Bottesford in June 1942. (IWM TR20)

Armourers bomb-up a Halifax of 405 Squadron on its dispersal at RAF Topcliffe.

Now that it is official that ops are planned, the crews go out to their dispersals to check on the serviceability of their aircraft, and if necessary fly air tests. The groundcrews busy themselves preparing the aircraft; tradesmen from the various sections check instruments, radar and electrical equipment; and the aircraft are fuelled, armed and bombed-up.

Late in the afternoon the aircrews file into the briefing room where they are told about their 'target for tonight'. The station intelligence officer (SIO) opens the briefing by unveiling the map to reveal the target for the night, with the route to be followed marked with red tape. Known flak and searchlight positions are also marked on this map by red and green celluloid overlays respectively. First, the SIO explains details of the target and why it has been chosen; he is followed by the signals, bombing and navigation leaders, who explain the various routines for the night. Next comes the flying control officer (FCO) who outlines engine start-up and marshalling times, and the runway to be used. Then the meteorological officer gives a full briefing on wind speeds, cloud and the weather likely to be encountered over the target. The squadron wing commanders follow by speaking to the crews in detail about the operation before handing over to the station commander who then wishes everyone good luck and a safe return.

With the briefing over, pilots obtain their maps for the night from the station map stores and mark onto them their proposed routes.

In the crew room at RAF Waterbeach the crew of a 99 Squadron Wellington struggle into their unwieldy Irvin two-piece flying suits before taking off for a night raid to Berlin, 9 April 1941. (IWM CH2505)

The wireless operators draw their 'flimsies' on which are printed radio frequencies and the signal colours of the day. Crews hurry to the parachute stores to collect chutes and Mae Wests, then make for the locker rooms where valuables are handed in and escape kits collected before changing into flying gear.

Amid the usual babble of conversation and the jumble of parachutes, helmets and flying boots, each man struggles into his unwieldy flying gear, the gunners usually taking the longest with their layers of electrically heated

Cigarette smoke and the smell of damp serge fill the air as Canadian Halifax bomber crews from 431 (Iroquois) and 434 (Bluenose) Squadrons are briefed for a raid on Essen.

This Lancaster of 44 Squadron sits patiently on its dispersal pan at RAF Dunholme Lodge, exuding latent power and menace, waiting for its crew to bring it to life before setting out for Berlin on 2 January 1944. (IWM CH11929)

clothing and the bulky Taylorsuits (see Glossary). Sandwiches and flasks of coffee for the return journey together with slabs of chocolate and barley sugar sweets are handed out to each crewmember from wrappings of newspaper.

Outside the locker room the buses arrive to take the crews on the short ride to their aircraft, dispersed around the perimeter of the airfield. A corporal stands at the open door shouting out the letters by which each aircraft is known. As space becomes available on a bus for that aircraft's crew, they climb on board and are taken out to their waiting aircraft.

After their pre-op briefing, Halifax crews of 76 Squadron climb on board their transports at RAF Holme-on-Spalding-Moor, Yorkshire, on 22 October 1943, to be driven out to the aircraft dispersals. Their target for tonight is the German city of Kassel. (IWM CH11401)

Once on their respective dispersals, each pilot completes the formalities of signing the Form 700 for the groundcrew corporal after a careful walk-around check of the control surfaces, wheel tyres and undercarriage oleo-legs. Then, after a last 'pee' on the dewy grass beside the dispersal, he and the rest of his crew board the aircraft: flight engineer, pilot, navigator, bomb-aimer and the wireless operator make their way up the fuselage to the nose, the two gunners to their turrets. The pilot stows his chute and straps himself into his seat. Outside in the dark on the dispersal pan the groundcrew move the battery starter trolley into position under the port wing.

The flight engineer checks to see that all the fuel cocks below his instrument panel are in their correct positions, then leans forward to the pilot and declares he is ready for engine start-up. The engineer looks out of the cockpit window and down to the ground beneath, calling back that the groundcrew are ready with their battery cart to start the port inner. When the pilot switches on the ignition, the fitter down beneath the wing shouts 'Contact!' The engineer presses one of the four black starter buttons on his panel and the first of four engines coughs, splutters and finally roars into life. The same procedure is repeated until all four engines are running. The pilot checks the intercom to all crew positions, then opens up the engines and allows them to warm up to operating temperature.

Taxiing times for each individual aircraft were set at briefing and the time to taxi out for take-off has now arrived. The engineer stands behind the pilot, keeping watch on the array of dials on his engineer's panel and the

Squadron Leader Alan Hobbs and crew board their 9 Squadron Lancaster on 20 June 1943. A ten-hour round trip to bomb Friedrichshafen lies ahead of them, one of the longest they will be expected to make. Six days later they were all dead, shot down over Holland by a night fighter.

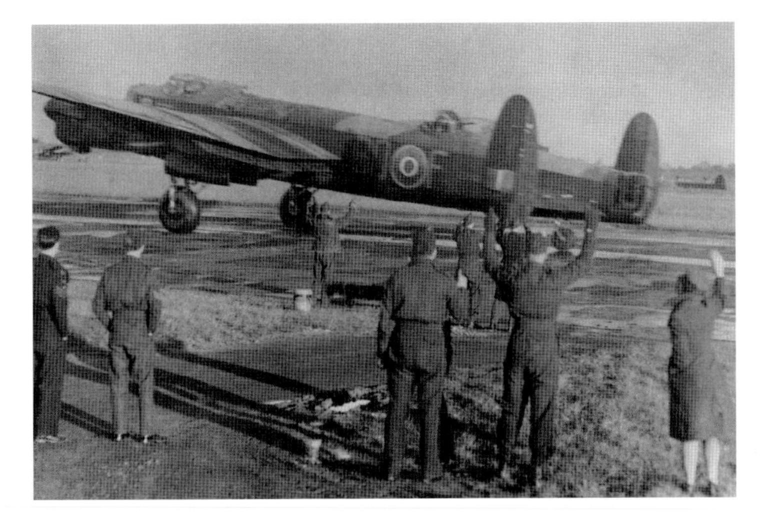

RAF and WAAF personnel wave to Flight Lieutenant D. A. Shaw and his 550 Squadron crew as they take off from RAF North Killingholme, bound for Bochum in Germany's Ruhr valley on 4 November 1944. Their Lancaster, 'F' for Freddie, is a rare beast because it is on its hundredth operational sortie. (IWM CH14188)

bomb-aimer comes up from his station in the nose to assist the pilot at take-off. The rear hatch door is secured by the groundcrew before the wheel chocks are pulled away and the pilot gently opens the throttles. On doughnut tyres the big bomber trundles and sways forward, following the aircraft in front around the perimeter track in slow procession towards the duty runway for the night, and joining the queue at the end. The pilot goes through his final cockpit check and the navigator outlines the flight plan and climb instructions. A green Aldis light flashes from the control van signalling to the pilot that it is his turn to line up for take-off.

With a full load of fuel and bombs, the bomber needs the full length of runway to get airborne. The pilot eases back on the control yoke and the bomber climbs slowly away into the night sky. Over the intercom the navigator gives the pilot a course to steer for their assembly point with other aircraft of the group, and with the reassuring red and green glow of navigation lights on the other aircraft in the sky all around them they soon leave the shores of England behind.

With a look of intense concentration etched on his face, this Short Stirling pilot eases his heavily laden bomber off the ground as the flight engineer (not visible in this picture) assists him with the throttles.

The gunners now request permission to test-fire their guns over the sea as the bomber continues to climb towards the briefed height for crossing the

ONE AIRMAN'S WAR: WING COMMANDER JOHN WOOLDRIDGE DSO, DFC, DFM (1919–58)

Born in Yokohama, Japan and educated at St Paul's School, London, John Wooldridge joined the RAF in 1938 as a sergeant pilot. By 1943 he had risen to become a wing commander, DSO, DFC, DFM, with a total of ninety-seven operational sorties over Germany to his credit. After service with 44, 76, 61 and 207 Squadrons, in 1942 he became a flight commander with 106 Squadron under Wing Commander Guy Gibson's command before being appointed CO of 105 Squadron in 1943. With this squadron Wooldridge became an expert in low-level precision daylight bombing, flying the de Havilland Mosquito. At this point he found time to write a book, *Low Attack* (Sampson Low, 1944), which is an authentic account of the operational activities of 105 and 139 Squadrons between 1940 and 1943.

After the war he left the RAF and devoted himself chiefly to the composition of music for the big screen. He also wrote the screenplay and score for *Appointment in London* (1953) starring Dirk Bogarde, a film portraying life on an RAF heavy bomber squadron during 1943. John Wooldridge's potentially high-flying career as a screenplay writer and composer was cut tragically short when he was killed in a car accident in 1958, aged thirty-nine.

enemy coast, now some ten minutes' flying time away. Continually scanning the sky for the first signs of enemy fighters, they swing their turrets from side to side. Behind the pilot, the flight engineer continues to monitor his instrument panel, checking fuel states, oil temperatures and pressures, and cross-feeding fuel when necessary. Meanwhile, the wireless operator tunes his set to listen in to the broadcast winds which come through at regular intervals. These are an average taken at group headquarters from meteorological data received from selected aircraft on the raid, and then rebroadcast to all aircraft to enable them to navigate using the same wind

Flying Officer P. Ingleby, the navigator of a 619 Squadron Lancaster, sits at his plotting table inside the curtained-off area behind the pilot. It was rare for a bomber navigator to venture out from his 'cubby hole' after take-off. (IWM CH12288)

speeds and directions. The navigator tunes the brilliance knob on his Gee set to get a comfortable picture, while down in the nose the bomb-aimer keeps a look-out for the enemy coast ahead, and the first puffs of flak coming up to greet them. (Gee was the codename for a passive radio navigation system

Bomb aimers had sufficient additional training to enable them to take over the flying controls from the pilot in an emergency. Flight Lieutenant P. Walmsley inside a Lancaster of 619 Squadron operates a Mk XIV Stabilised Vector Bombsight, one of two main sights used by Bomber Command. (IWM CH12283)

used by the RAF that helped improve bomber crews' navigation accuracy.) Passing through the 5,000ft height band the order comes from the pilot to switch on oxygen.

After the enemy coast has been crossed, the navigator gives the pilot a new course to steer that will take them to the target, with an estimated time of arrival. It is about thirty to forty minutes' flying time from the Dutch coast to the Ruhr, but more than two hours to a more distant target like Berlin. The gently waving fingers of searchlights continue to probe the night sky as the bomber drones on its course to the target.

The Lancaster crews of 100 Group 'jam' the German fighter controllers and radar sets with special electronic gadgets, which keeps the enemy guessing where the bombers will finally strike. Ahead of the main bomber force, the Pathfinders drop coloured route and target markers. The heavy flak guns open up with a vengeance as they begin to mark the target with their red flares.

Now that the pilot has turned onto the final leg to the target, the bomb-aimer goes down to his station in the nose to check his bombsight and fusing panel; the engineer checks the master fuel cocks; the wireless operator pushes bundles of 'Window' (see Glossary) down the flare chute to confuse enemy radar; the pilot calls up the gunners to keep their eyes peeled for enemy fighters; and the navigator's voice comes over the intercom to give the pilot their time to target. Each member of the crew is busy as the aircraft begins its final run-in to the target.

This would have been a familiar sight to RAF bomber crews from out of their cockpits and gun turrets. This Lancaster is silhouetted against the smoke and explosions during a raid on Hamburg on the night of 30/31 January 1943. (IWM C3371)

With the bomb doors now open, the pilot holds the bomber straight and level for its bombing run. Beneath them the target area is a sea of flame, punctuated by the red and green target markers dropped by the Pathfinders. Dozens of searchlight beams grope the sky, hoping to illuminate a bomber so that the flak batteries can blast it from the sky. The crew can hear the occasional dull thud of a shell bursting close by, and perhaps the clattering on the fuselage as pieces of spent shrapnel hit them.

The bomb-aimer directs the pilot with calm instructions of 'Left, left, steady, right a bit. Hold it there, left a bit. Bombs gone!' The aircraft seems to rear up in the sky, relieved of her heavy cargo of bombs, but the pilot needs to fly straight and level for

ONE AIRMAN'S WAR: SERGEANT LESLIE FRY, FLIGHT ENGINEER, 429 (RCAF) SQUADRON (1922–44)

In 1944, 22-year-old Sergeant Leslie Fry from Ramsgate, Kent, was a Handley Page Halifax flight engineer on 429 Squadron RCAF. He was the sole Englishman in a crew of seven; this was typical of the practice in Canadian bomber squadrons where the RAF trained and supplied them with flight engineers. Fry had completed his engineer training in April 1944 with 4 School of Technical Training at St Athan. He was crewed-up in May on 1666 Heavy Conversion Unit at Wombleton in Yorkshire before he was posted to 429 (RCAF) Squadron at Leeming (also in Yorkshire) in July.

On their twelfth op on 24 September, Fry and his crew were shot down by flak during a daylight attack on the German garrison at the French Channel port of Calais. The bomb-aimer bailed out and was killed before the Halifax crash-landed in a nearby wood. Miraculously, the rest of the crew walked away with cuts and bruises.

They returned to operations the following month and on 30 November Fry and his crew were briefed for a night attack on the Ruhr city of Duisberg, which would be their seventeenth op. In a complicated plan that involved 576 heavy bombers flying two separate routes into Germany, at varying heights and in pitch darkness, the attacking force was to be streamed over the target within fourteen minutes.

Some 40 miles short of the target, Fry's Halifax collided over Holland with another Halifax bomber, from 578 Squadron. All fourteen men from the two crews died. With such a complicated flight plan it was an accident waiting to happen. Between July 1942 and May 1945, Bomber Command lost approximately 112 aircraft through collision – amounting to more than 700 aircrew.

another thirty seconds to enable the aiming point photograph to be taken. Without it their operation will not count towards their tour of thirty operations. With the enemy defences now well awakened and throwing all they can at the slowly moving bomber stream overhead, most crews see this as the longest 30 seconds of their lives. Before they

The relief on the faces of this 51 Squadron Halifax crew is plain to see as they hand in their parachutes to a WAAF at RAF Snaith in Yorkshire. They have just returned from a raid on the Nazi industrial heartland of the Ruhr (known to bomber crews as 'Happy Valley') in June 1943. (IWM CH10293)

can leave the target area, the bomb-aimer checks on his control panel for signs of any bomb hang-ups (unreleased bombs inside the bomb bay), which could mean another run over the target, but if all is well the bomb doors are closed and they turn for home.

Vigilance is still required on the long haul back across blacked-out Europe to the enemy coast. Flak and searchlights are still active and German nightfighters loiter for the unwary crew who have let down their guard now

Safely back from ops, these 149 Squadron crews pause for well-earned mugs of tea laced with rum, a cigarette and a chat, before their debriefing from the intelligence officer at RAF Lakenheath in the spring of 1944. (IWM CH12689)

that the tension of the bomb run has passed, or the one that has lost its way from the relative safety of the bomber stream. Some, even, have been shot down on the home straight by enemy intruders lurking in the circuit at their base as they prepare to land.

Once across the enemy coast and over the sea, the navigator picks up his Gee lattice line and they join the procession that will lead to home. In a short while, 50 miles from the English coast, the pilot calls up on VHF and identifies his aircraft. Once over England, the crew look out below for the Pundit beacon that flashes in Morse code the identification letters of their home airfield. A call is then made to the control tower asking for permission to join the circuit and land.

Safely back on the ground, the engines are shut down and the exhausted crew climb out of their aircraft and are taken by crew bus to debriefing. They answer a lengthy questionnaire giving details of the operation they have just flown. Welcome mugs of tea and much needed cigarettes help the crew to unwind before they return their flying kit to the stores and lockers and retire to their billets for a well-earned sleep.

Squadron Leader J. Martin's 622 Squadron Stirling crew relate their experiences to an intelligence officer at RAF Mildenhall, Suffolk, on their return from the major raid against Berlin of 22/23 November 1943. (IWM CH11641)

ADVICE TO THE RELATIVE OF A MAN WHO IS MISSING

In view of the official notification that your relative is missing, you will naturally wish to hear what is being done to trace him.

The Service Departments make every endeavour to discover the fate of missing men, and draw upon all likely sources of information about them.

A man who is missing after an engagement may possibly be a prisoner of war. Continuous efforts are made to speed up the machinery whereby the names and camp addresses of prisoners of war can reach this country. The official means is by lists of names prepared by the enemy Government. These lists take some time to compile, especially if there is a long journey from the place of capture to a prisoners of war camp. Consequently "capture cards" filled in by the prisoners themselves soon after capture and sent home to their relatives are often the first news received in this country that a man is a prisoner of war. That is why you are asked in the accompanying letter to forward at once any card or letter you may receive, if it is the first news you have had.

Even if no news is received that a missing man is a prisoner of war, endeavours to trace him do not cease. Enquiries are pursued not only among those

LUCK AND COURAGE

THE GRIM REALITIES of operational flying put the survival prospects for RAF bomber crews into sharp perspective. In 1942 less than half of all heavy bomber crews would survive their first tour; one in five would live to survive a second. By 1943 the odds against survival had lengthened further still with one in six expected to survive their first tour, while a slim one in forty would survive two tours.

Based on the British Army's combat experience in the First World War, the RAF in the Second World War soon realised that in order to sustain a bomber offensive over a long period of time some form of front-line crew rotation would be necessary. At first two hundred hours of operational flying was established by the Air Ministry as the cut-off point after which a bomber crew could be taken off operations (or 'ops') and rested (or 'screened' – no longer compelled to fly operationally) at a flying training unit.

In 1941 the notion of an absolute number of operations constituting a 'tour of duty' came into being: thirty sorties, not exceeding two hundred flying hours, was regarded as sufficient for completion of a heavy bomber tour, with a six-month break from operations at a flying training establishment followed by a second tour. Pathfinder Force crews committed themselves to a tour of forty-five sorties.

Aircrew survival depended upon various factors, which included the operational experience of a crew, their degree of alertness and vigilance when flying, the type of aircraft they were flying, whether day or night operations were being flown, the year of the war in which they were operating – and luck.

If a crew was to stand a fair chance of survival, the aircraft in which they were flying had a strong bearing on the outcome. The Avro Lancaster came top of the RAF's trio of heavy bombers. But if a crew was unlucky and needed to bail out, then the Lanc was more difficult to exit quickly and successfully than either the Handley Page Halifax or the Short Stirling. Conversely, the Halifax and Stirling suffered greater losses than the Lancaster, and the Stirling in particular was eventually withdrawn from frontline operations in late 1943 because of unsustainable casualties.

Opposite: Official advice to the next of kin of RAF aircrew posted missing. Although the leaflet offers reassurance that all possible lines of enquiry were being followed up to discover the fate of a man, the sad reality was that most bomber crewmen were dead by the time their aircraft hit the ground.

Another op completed, the chance to see another dawn. Flight Lieutenant A. Carey leads his 102 Squadron Halifax crew to the interrogation room at RAF Pocklington, Yorkshire, on their return from a night raid on Frankfurt-am-Main on 4/5 October 1943. (IWM CH11234)

Once a heavy bomber crew had completed twelve operations, their chances of going on to complete a full tour of thirty ops without becoming casualties was good. To improve their chances of survival, they might have taken some of the following precautions: observing strict R/T (radio-telephony) procedure; flying a gently weaving course to and from the target, rather than remaining straight and level for long periods; banking the aircraft from side to side to enable the gunners to check the blind spots beneath the wings for an enemy fighter that might be moving into position for attack; gunners keeping a constant look-out for enemy nightfighters, continually scanning the night sky while traversing their turrets from side to side; and maintaining a high level of concentration on the way home from the target, when the temptation was to relax.

The Ball family lost three of their five sons serving in Bomber Command. Leslie and Peter (pictured) were both pilots: Sergeant Leslie failed to return from ops on 21 November 1940, Flying Officer Peter (DFM) on 5 August 1942. Their brother Ken was killed on active service in 1942.

It was all the more perplexing, therefore, when a crew that followed all of these precautions suddenly 'failed to return' one night. There was no simple explanation, but many crews took a fatalistic view and put it down to the luck of the draw.

All RAF bomber aircrew were volunteers, but this process did not work in reverse; this meant that an individual could not 'volunteer out' if flying was not to his liking, if the pressures were too great or if he later found himself psychologically unsuited to flying duties.

It was difficult for aircrew to move around the interior of a bomber; but it was even more troublesome in pitch darkness, with the pilot 'corkscrewing' the aircraft around the sky to evade an attacking night fighter. This is the inside of a Lancaster looking forward.

The tremendous strains of operational flying imposed on bomber aircrew affected all men to greater or lesser degrees, but there were some who took it worse than others. Operational twitch, loss of nerve, emotional exhaustion, shell-shock – it took many forms and as many

Instructions on how to bail out a wounded crewman from a Lancaster with the use of a static line to release his parachute. His flying helmet was removed to prevent strangulation during the descent.

This bomber crew had a lucky escape after their aircraft was attacked by a night fighter. An RAF heavy bomber pilot's standard fighter evasion manoeuvre was the 'corkscrew'. The constant changes in direction, speed and altitude of this manoeuvre proved highly effective. (IWM CH12690)

descriptions – was not entertained by those in positions of authority within the RAF.

The official term was 'Lack of Moral Fibre' (simply abbreviated to LMF) and those branded as such were humiliated and vilified by the RAF before being drummed out of the service. LMF was thought to be contagious and had to be dealt with swiftly to avoid 'contamination', so an 'infected' man was posted off a bomber station immediately. Aircrew officers were often

Death for a bomber crew could come just as easily from one's own side as from the enemy. Here two crewmembers of 115 Squadron's Lancaster 'L' for Leather examine the rear of their aircraft, where the rear turret, with its unfortunate gunner, was sheared off by bombs dropped from another aircraft in 1943. (IWM CE79)

CONFIDENTIAL NOTICE

The names of all who lose their lives or are wounded or reported missing while serving with the Royal Air Force will appear in the official casualty lists published from time to time in the Press.

Any publication of the date, place or circumstances of a casualty, and particularly any reference to the unit concerned, might give valuable information to the enemy, and for this reason, only the name, rank and Service number are included in the official lists.

Relatives are particularly requested, in the national interest, to ensure that any notices published privately do not disclose the date, place or circumstances of the casualty, or the unit.

The Press have been asked to co-operate in ensuring that no information of value to the enemy is published.

[OVER

(C50819) 20,000 11/43

Any premature reference in the Press to those reported missing may jeopardise their chances of evading capture, if they have survived without falling into enemy hands.

Relatives of missing bomber aircrew were asked not to divulge operational details in any death notices published in the press. Failure of newspaper editors to comply with the Government's rules on self-censorship could mean closure of a newspaper and imprisonment for its editor.

cashiered (dismissed in disgrace), and NCO aircrew were reduced to the ranks or discharged from the service altogether; some were transferred to either the Army or the Navy, or were sent down the coal mines as 'Bevin Boys'.

By the standards of the twenty-first century, the punishment dispensed to those who could no longer take the strain of operations was harsh and inhumane, the intention being to prevent others of questionable morale from trying to avoid combat duties. Nevertheless, the RAF was loath to court-martial a man accused of LMF for fear of the adverse publicity such a trial might generate. In fact some high-ranking officers and politicians, including the Secretary of State for Air, considered parts of the LMF policy were indefensible from a popular point of view.

When compared with the USAAF's more enlightened view that most LMF cases were psychological in origin and should therefore be treated medically, the RAF's policy, based as it was on its questionable views on character deficiency and cowardice, was more harsh and designed to act as a deterrent.

The policy's harshness accounts for the comparatively small number of LMF cases

One-sixth of Bomber Command's wartime fatalities (more than 8,000) were sustained during training. 'Pilot Officer Prune', the fictitious dim-witted protagonist of *Tee Emm*, the 'classified' RAF aircrew training publication, was used to demonstrate humorously to aircrews how not to do it.

FIDO (Fog Investigation Dispersal Operations) petrol burners are ignited at RAF Graveley as a Lancaster takes off in deteriorating weather. By the winter of 1944 this life-saving device had enabled more than 1,000 Allied aircraft to make safe landings despite dense fog. (IWM CH15271)

in Bomber Command during the Second World War, which ran at approximately 200 per year, although surviving records are not sufficiently comprehensive to confirm this figure. However, the true figure is probably higher because many aircrew who experienced psychological problems associated with combat flying, but who were fearful of being branded LMF, kept their fears bottled up and either completed their tours – or simply failed to return. Some should never have continued to fly because their state of mind made them a liability to their crew. Yet at no time in the war was the problem of LMF significant enough to compromise Bomber Command's operational effectiveness, even during the Battles of the Ruhr and Berlin in 1943–4 when casualties among aircrew ran high.

During the Second World War 10,995 RAF bomber crewmen were taken prisoners of war. They were the lucky ones, for the chances of getting out of a crashing bomber and surviving were slim indeed. Flying in an RAF heavy bomber was akin to riding a giant explosive device. Laden with bombs and high octane fuel, oxygen tanks and thousands of rounds of ammunition, a bomber was liable to explode instantly when shot at by an attacking night fighter, or when hit by flak. If the bomber survived the initial attack, then the negative 'g' force exerted when it spun earthwards out of control usually trapped many airmen inside.

Not all those who survived being shot down went 'into the bag' (as prisoner of war camps were known to their allied inmates). Some 2,138 RAF

airmen who came down in enemy territory either evaded capture or escaped from captivity. Many returned home via the various escape networks in Occupied Europe to rejoin their units and fight again.

The dead crew of an RAF Halifax have been laid out next to the wreckage of their aircraft. They were shot down and killed by the German defences near Delmenhorst, on their way to bomb Hamburg on 3 February 1943. (IWM HU25782)

This surviving crewmember from a 158 Squadron Halifax, who was shot down over Bremen in the evening of 27 March 1943 while flying to bomb Berlin, is interrogated by Luftwaffe officers. (IWM HU25790)

DRESSED FOR ACTION

UNIFORMS

Both officers' and airmen's blue-grey tunics were worn on operations by bomber crews from the beginning of the war, either on their own or beneath a flying suit, until largely superseded by the battledress in 1941.

The airman's uniform was an off-the-peg garment made from coarse and itchy unlined serge, which was much less comfortable to wear than the tailored and lined officer's barathea version. Different styles of uniform were worn by personnel of the Dominions and air forces in exile, serving alongside their RAF comrades in Bomber Command. They retained the uniforms and insignia of their own national air forces, for example: Australia (dark blue), South Africa (brown) and Free French (black). However, the uniforms of the RCAF and Polish Air Force, for example, were identical to the RAF pattern except for buttons and insignia.

The RAF No. 1 dress tunic, as worn by commissioned officers and warrant officers (WO) during the Second World War, dates from 1919 and was based on the Army cavalry officer's tunic, with rank displayed on the cuffs according to Royal Navy tradition.

Made from fine blue-grey barathea woollen cloth, the No. 1 dress uniform was worn with blue-grey shirt and black tie and comprised a tunic and trousers, with black lace-up shoes. The quality and cut of the uniform depended very much on what you were able to pay. Headgear was either the service dress peaked cap or field service side cap, both in blue-grey.

The blue-grey serge unlined open-neck tailored four-pocket tunic and trousers was issued from 1936 to all airmen up to and including the rank of flight sergeant (including air and groundcrews during the Second World War). It too was worn with a blue-grey shirt and black tie, with black lace-up shoes. A field service side cap in blue-grey serge was worn with this uniform for everyday use.

The 'suit, blue-grey, aircrews' – otherwise known as battledress – was introduced in 1941 for the sole use of RAF flying personnel when flying, but later became available for wear by all RAF personnel. Modelled on the British

Opposite: These two RCAF Halifax crewmen each wear a Life Jacket Mk I 'Mae West' over their battledress tops. The flight lieutenant on the right wears 1940-pattern flying boots and 1941-pattern flying gauntlets.

Right: In 1939, the five-man Armstrong Whitworth Whitley was classed as a heavy bomber and was produced in far greater quantities than its mediocre performance merited.

Below: An officer's side cap with brass albatross and crown. These caps were made out of fine barathea woollen cloth, while those of non-commissioned aircrew were made from serge .

Below right: This RAF issue button escape compass was one of several ingenious gadgets designed to help shot-down RAF aircrew. The button was undone by a left-hand thread to reveal a tiny compass. (IWM EPH3604)

Army battledress, it was made from blue-grey serge and comprised a blouse and trousers. The blouse was fastened at the front with concealed buttons and a side-fastening buckle at the waist. It also featured button-down epaulettes, two large pleated patch pockets and was worn unbuttoned at the neck to reveal collar and tie. The aircrew whistle (for use in the event of ditching or being shot down, to attract the attention of fellow crewmembers) was worn only with the battledress and was attached to the collar fastener. The trousers had buttons at the ankles to enable them to be fastened more

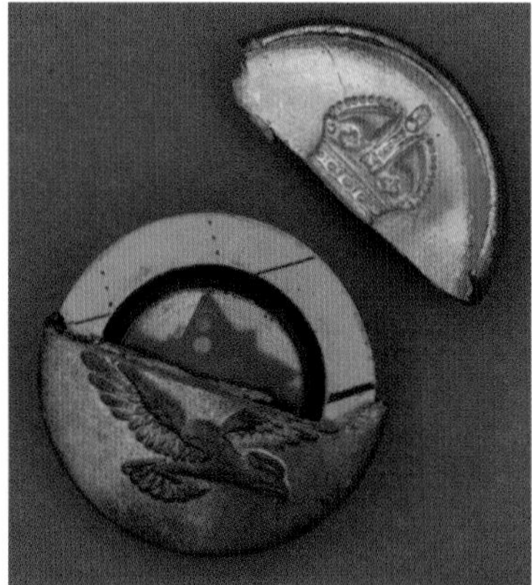

RAF headgear badges and tunic buttons. From left to right: warrant officer, airman and officer cap badges. In the foreground are tunic (brass) and battledress (black plastic) buttons.

To aid an airman who had been shot down and was on the run, these 1943 Pattern 'Escape' flying boots could easily be converted into 'civilian' lace-up shoes by cutting off the black suede uppers. Inside the right boot is a concealed pocket that contains a small knife for this purpose. (IWM UNI12092)

Canadian Pilot Officer S. Jess, wireless operator of a Lancaster bomber operating from RAF Waddington, Lincolnshire, carrying two pigeon boxes. Homing pigeons served as a means of communication in the event of a crash, ditching into the sea or radio failure. (IWM TR193)

tightly to fit into flying boots. The same battledress pattern was issued to both officers and other ranks. Headgear was the same for officers' or airmen's dress as noted above.

INSIGNIA

Both commissioned and non-commissioned ranks wore their flying brevets and medal ribbons above the left breast pocket. Aircrew in 8 (Pathfinder) Group wore the gilt Pathfinder badge on the left breast pocket flap below the medal ribbons, but not on operations for obvious security reasons. Where applicable, brass 'VR' (volunteer reserve) collar studs were worn by officers on each lapel; these were discontinued in mid-1943. Cloth national identity flashes – for example 'CANADA' – were applied to each shoulder. There were forty-two such empire titles authorised for use.

Flying Officer George Pelter was a navigator on Halifaxes with 425 (Alouette) Squadron, RCAF. He wears the RAF officers' No. 1 dress uniform with the early war 'O' observer brevet over his left breast pocket, and has 'CANADA' flashes on each shoulder.

NCO and airmen's rank distinctions were worn on each arm, embroidered warrant officers' crowns on the sleeve of each forearm. Airmen's trade badges were worn on the right sleeve only. The RAF

Flight Lieutenant Joe McCarthy and his 617 Squadron crew are wearing battledress. Flying brevets and medal ribbons are worn above the left breast pocket, personal name tags above the right. Sergeants' stripes are worn on the right sleeve only, officers' rank braid on both epaulettes. (IWM TR1128)

eagle arm badge worn by all non-commissioned airmen below warrant officer rank was applied to each shoulder, together with cloth national identity flashes and cloth VR badges.

On battledress, officers' rank insignia was worn on each shoulder strap, but airmen's and warrant officers' rank badges were worn on the right arm only. Flying brevets, medal ribbons and the Pathfinder badge were worn as for the No. 1 dress and airmen's tunic.

During the Second World War the RAF awarded 20,000 DFCs for officers, and 6,600 DFMs for NCO aircrew. The medals shown belonged to Flight Lieutenant David Shannon, RAAF, who flew with the famous 617 Squadron (the dam busters). They include the Distinguished Service Order and the DFC, both with Bars. (IWM OMD3906)

FLYING CLOTHING AND EQUIPMENT

Apart from the ever-vigilant German defences and the unpredictability of the weather, the bomber crew's other enemy was the cold. Flying high to avoid enemy defences meant that aircrews needed additional protection against freezing temperatures, particularly in aircraft that had no effective cabin heating systems, and at heights above 10,000 feet they also needed to breathe more oxygen.

With increasing altitude there is a corresponding drop in air pressure, air temperature and oxygen content of the atmosphere (1.98°C drop in temperature for every 1,000 feet up to 36,000 feet, after which it is assumed to remain constant at -56°C). Unassisted breathing above this height becomes progressively laboured unless wearing an oxygen mask, without which unconsciousness and death follow swiftly.

In the first year of the war most RAF bomber operations were flown below 10,000 feet and therefore below oxygen height, and at this altitude extreme cold was seldom encountered. But as the German defences became more of a threat, and heavier, more powerful bombers came into service with Bomber Command, the operating heights increased and with them the need for heated flying clothing and special breathing apparatus.

Protection from the cold for RAF aircrews – of which Bomber Command crews were the main beneficiaries – was solved by the backroom boffins at RAE Farnborough and in private industry. Their solutions included

These Stirling crewmembers wear various items of flying kit: the pilot (third from left) wears an Irvin sheepskin jacket over battledress; the two gunners (standing, right) wear 1941-pattern Sidcot suits, wired for electrically heated clothing. The man in the foreground wears a leather jacket. Five of them wear parachute harnesses and Mae Wests.

a range of thermally insulated and electrically heated flying suits, jackets and trousers, including specialy designed flying helmets, boots, gloves and socks, which gave protection to the bodily extremities most prone to frostbite.

This H-Type high altitude oxygen mask with built-in microphone would have been used by de Havilland Mosquito bomber crews and high-flying photo reconnaissance pilots in the last year of the war.

Freezing temperatures were the enemy of the bomber crewman. Heated specialist flying clothing was developed for Bomber Command crews, including these D-Type leather flying gloves.

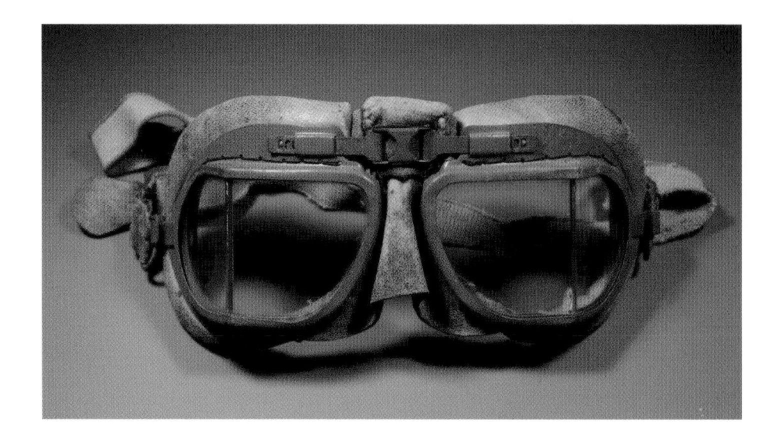

Introduced in October 1943, the Mk VIII flying goggles featured two-piece lenses in a streamlined grey metal frame backed with leather cushioning. They were the last goggles to be issued to aircrews before the RAF introduced 'bone domes' and wrap-around visors in the late 1950s.

To facilitate breathing at altitude a simple oxygen delivery system was devised in 1935 to pipe oxygen from a pressurised bottle and into a face mask worn by the airman. Although an improvement on what had gone before – that is to say, nothing – this constant-flow method of delivery was quickly found to be wasteful and led to the invention of what was termed the 'economiser flow system', which eventually became a standard fit in the RAF's heavy bombers. The economiser system meant that oxygen was released from the bottled supply only when the wearer of the oxygen mask actually inhaled. Improved flying clothing and oxygen delivery systems continued to be developed through the war years.

CREW INTER-COMMUNICATIONS

A vital piece of equipment for the RAF bomber crew was the aircraft's internal communication (intercom) system, to which all crewmembers were connected for the purpose of speaking to one another. The oxygen masks they wore fulfilled a dual function, not only helping the wearer to breathe at altitude, but also enabling him to speak to his fellow crewmembers with the aid of a built-in microphone connected by a lead to the intercom system.

To allow RAF crews to listen in to both external radio transmissions and inter-crew conversations, a small earphone was wired into each earpiece of the flying helmet. If the

Opposite bottom: This C-Type helmet, Mk VIII flying goggles and G-Type oxygen mask are worn by Sergeant W. Brown, a Stirling mid-upper gunner with 199 Squadron in mid-1944.

Left: The C-Type chrome leather flying helmet of the mid- to late-Second World War period was used extensively by RAF bomber crewmen.

intercom system failed completely owing to damage from enemy action, or occasionally because of equipment malfunction, it was not difficult for the crews in a Lancaster, Halifax or Mosquito to exchange handwritten notes to maintain contact.

Both British- and American-built bomber aircraft were equipped with 'call lights' where each crew position was provided with a small unit fitted with three coloured light bulbs and three buttons. In the event of an intercom failure a signalling procedure worked out in advance enabled crewmembers to communicate with one another, although the captain always had priority. It was a vital back-up system, particularly for the tail gunner in heavy bombers, if the pilot ordered his crew to abandon aircraft.

STAYING WARM

The coldest crew position in wartime heavy bomber aircraft was usually that of the gunners, particularly in the rear turret. Although the internal heating systems of bomber aircraft like the Halifax and Lancaster worked fairly effectively in the forward ends of the fuselage, they were none the less rudimentary affairs and not to be wholly relied upon. In the Lancaster, for example, the heating duct outlet was adjacent to the wireless operator's position, so he and the navigator were invariably hot. But while he and the navigator might be working in shirtsleeves or battledress, on the other side

Wing Commander Reggie Reynolds (right) and his navigator, Flight Lieutenant Ted Sismore, wear B-Type and C-Type flying helmets respectively. The former helmet was standard issue to all RAF aircrew between 1936 and 1941. Reynolds and Sismore also wear Mae Wests over their battledress. (IWM CH10135)

of the blackout curtain, which shut off the navigator's compartment from the cockpit area, the pilot, flight engineer and bomb-aimer froze. It was a similar story aft of the main spar where the mid-upper and rear gunners could be shivering in their turrets in temperatures of -40°C, despite being wrapped up against the cold in five layers of thermally insulated and electrically heated flying clothing, boots and gloves. At the war's end about half the Lancaster force had been equipped with ducted heating to the rear turret, but Halifax aircraft rear turrets remained unheated.

The canary-yellow Taylor buoyant suit introduced in 1942 went some way towards improving the lot of the air gunner, but if worn with electrically heated linings the circuitry in this kind of flying clothing was inclined to play up on a fairly regular basis. It was not unknown for some wearers to suffer skin burns due to electrical short circuits, the first indication of which was a smell of burning.

The Mosquito bomber crews of Bomber Command's 2, 5, 8 and 100 Groups were blessed with very effective cabin heating in their aircraft, so much so that even during winter months on high-level sorties they only needed to wear Sidcot suits (see Glossary) over battledress to keep warm. In the summer, however, the cockpit could become uncomfortably hot due to the greenhouse effect of the perspex cockpit canopy.

MAE WESTS

Yellow RAF aircrew bouyancy jackets were a distinctive feature of bomber crew flying kit. Popularly referred to as 'Mae Wests' owing to their similarity to the ample bosoms of the American film star of the same name, they were intended to help airmen stay afloat whose aircraft had come down in water. The jackets came in two patterns – the relatively old-fashioned 1932-pattern Life Jacket, and the Life Jacket Mk I (1941).

The Mae West was a thick khaki cotton twill waistcoat containing an inflatable rubber air bladder, fastened at the front with three buttons and two buckled straps. The front panels were often painted yellow by bomber crewmen to make the wearer more visible in the water. The Life Jacket Mk I, which became RAF standard issue from 1941, was also dull yellow in colour but the air bladder was now inflated by a break-neck CO_2 cylinder.

The seven-man crew of a Lancaster wait near the crew room at RAF Waddington, Lincolnshire, for transport out to their aircraft, October 1942. They wear Mae Wests and their parachute packs are lying on the grass in the foreground. Inside the yellow boxes are homing pigeons. (IWM TR186)

EPILOGUE: BACK ON CIVVY STREET

As the war drew to a close in Europe, over the six years of war Bomber Command crews had flown a total of 387,416 sorties and dropped more than 955,000 tons of bombs. By the time VE Day arrived, it had already

This Halifax of 10 Squadron was one of the last RAF bomber aircraft of the war to be lost on operations, 9 April 1945. It crashed outside the municipal offices in Dusseldorf, killing five of its crew and injuring two others. (IWM CL2444)

begun to wind down its huge organisation. The number of trainee aircrew began to decline during 1944 and more than a third of the bomber training units had closed before the war's end. After VE Day, most of Bomber Command's aircrew were demobilised and began returning to their lives and jobs on 'Civvy Street'. The 10,000 bomber crewmen who had been prisoners of war in Germany and Occupied Europe were repatriated to their home countries – most of them being carried home in Bomber Command Lancasters and Halifaxes.

Many found it hard to make the transition from tight-knit bomber crew to the mundane routines of civilian life in office, shop or factory. The seemingly pointless nature of so much in civilian life jarred with the intensity of their existence over the past few years when their very survival hung in the balance.

Some men chose to continue flying, joining commercial airlines like BOAC and British South American Airways. The latter had been founded in 1945 by ex-Pathfinder chief, Don Bennett, and its first aircraft were converted bombers mainly flown by former Bomber Command men.

There were other bomber crewmen who chose to remain in the air force during its post-war transition to a peacetime service; some were tempted

In the closing weeks of the war, bomber crews became involved in air-dropping supplies to the starving population of Holland – codenamed 'Operation Manna'. Here, groundcrew prepare to load sacks of food into the bomb-bay of a Lancaster of 514 Squadron at RAF Waterbeach, Cambridgeshire, on 29 April 1945. (IWM CL2489)

to stay on by offers of permanent commissions. Many who stayed were posted to RAF Transport Command, flying Avro Yorks and Douglas Dakotas to the far corners of a now shrinking Empire.

However, the peacetime RAF was a very different animal from its wartime counterpart. Its high commanders sought a quick return to the discipline and order of the pre-war RAF, and the rapid promotion enjoyed by many in the war years was now a far slower affair.

But what of those bomber crewmen who never made it home? From a force of 125,000 men, some 55,000 Bomber Command aircrew were killed on operations and in training accidents, and 8,953 aircraft were lost. These fallen airmen lie buried in cemeteries across Europe and in the counties of eastern England. More than 22,000 bomber crewmen disappeared without trace over land and ocean. These men have no known graves and are commemorated on the Allied Air Forces Memorial at Runnymede in Surrey.

In the years that followed the war, many British politicians – including Winston Churchill – tried to distance themselves from what they considered to be the distasteful nature of the allied bomber offensive. Former bomber crewmen felt betrayed by this sudden change in attitude.

Germany's towns and cities were wrecked by the intensity of allied bombing. This low- level aerial photograph of the devastated city centre of Stuttgart was taken weeks after the war ended in May 1945. (IWM CL3437)

With the war over, Bomber Command began to demobilise. Thinking of life back on 'Civvy Street', these two airmen select hats to go with their demob suits at a civilian clothing centre in Wembley. (IWM CH18633)

The policy of strategic bombing in the Second World War, its effectiveness in defeating Nazi Germany and the morality of the area bombing

Gram churchyard in Denmark is the final resting place of Flying Officer Jim Murray, RNZAF, and three of his 75 (New Zealand) Squadron Stirling crew, shot down by a night fighter as they returned from a mine-laying sortie in Kiel Bay in 1944.

campaign, remain hotly debated issues to this day. What cannot ever be denied, though, is the bravery of the RAF's bomber crewmen. Their courage and resolve through some of the most gruelling combat conditions in the history of warfare has become legendary.

Above: Bomber Command crews were eligible for a number of Second World War campaign medals. The Air Crew Europe Star was awarded to British and Commonwealth aircrew for at least two months' operational flying over Europe between 3 September 1939 and 5 June 1944.

Right: 'Bomber' Harris, the wartime commander of RAF Bomber Command, is commemorated by a statue placed outside St Clement Danes RAF church in central London.

GLOSSARY AND ABBREVIATIONS

Bomb dump Area at the edge of an airfield where bombs were stored.

Bomber stream As many aircraft as possible were funnelled over a given point in the shortest time possible to swamp enemy defences.

Corkscrew Bomber aircraft's evasive manoeuvre.

FCO Flying Control Officer.

Flak German anti-aircraft artillery (from the German *Fliegerabwehrkanone*).

Flare path System of runway lighting that lines the edges of a runway to assist flying operations at night and in poor visibility.

Form 700 Aircraft service log kept by groundcrew and signed by the pilot before a flight as his acceptance that the plane is fit for use.

Gee Passive radio navigational aid.

Goodwood Also called 'maximum effort', when a bomber squadron is ordered to mobilise all aircraft and crews for a raid.

H-hour Start time of an operation, or take-off time.

H2S Air-to-ground mapping radar.

Intercom Aircraft's internal communication (intercom) system.

LMF Lack of moral fibre.

Luftwaffe German Air Force.

Mae West Aircrew life preserver for use in event of forced landing in water.

Mandrel screen Electronic jamming of enemy early warning radar.

NCO Non-commissioned officer, such as a sergeant.

Oboe Distance-measuring navigational aid using pulsed radio transmissions.

Ops Operations.

OTU Operational Training Unit.

Pathfinder RAF's specialist target marking force.

Perspex Tough transparent plastic material used for window glazing in aircraft.

Popsy Single woman or girlfriend.

Pundit beacon Automatic red-light beacon flashing airfield's identification code letters in Morse.

RAAF Royal Australian Air Force.

RAFVR Royal Air Force Volunteer Reserve.

RCAF Royal Canadian Air Force.

RCM Radio countermeasures.

RNZAF Royal New Zealand Air Force.
R/T Radio telephony.
Sidcot suit One-piece lightweight overall-type flying suit.
SIO Station Intelligence Officer.
Taylorsuit Heavy, electrically heated, buoyant flying suit for air gunners.
Tour Thirty operations for a main force bomber crew, forty-five for a Pathfinder crew.
USAAF United States Army Air Force.
WAG Wireless operator/air gunner.
Window Strips of foil-backed paper dropped in clumps from RAF bombers to confuse enemy radar; the RAF's single most important RCM device of the war.

The aircrew of 88 Squadron at RAF Attlebridge, Norfolk, stand around a bomb-trolley carrying 500lb bombs that are about to be loaded into Douglas Bostons, May 1942. (IWM CH5595)

FURTHER READING

GENERAL HISTORIES

Bishop, Patrick. *Bomber Boys*. Harper Press, 2007.

Hastings, Max. *Bomber Command*. Pan, 1999.

Middlebrook, Martin. *The Bomber Command War Diaries*. Midland, 2006.

THE COMMANDERS

Bennett, Don. *Pathfinder*. Goodall, 1998.

Harris, Arthur. *Bomber Offensive*. Pen and Sword, 2005.

AIRCREW ACCOUNTS

Charlwood, Don. *No Moon Tonight*. Goodall, 2000.

Currie, Jack. *Lancaster Target*. Goodall, 2004.

Rolfe, Mel. *Flying into Hell: The Bomber Command Offensive as Recorded by the Crews Themselves*. Grub Street, 2008.

Tripp, Miles. *The Eighth Passenger*. Wordsworth, 2002.

A page from the *ABC of the RAF* for children, showing that Bomber Command's tail gunners were always keen for a good scrap with the enemy. What it doesn't say is that the tail gunner had the coldest and the most dangerous crew position in a bomber aircraft.

KEY RAIDS

Falconer, Jonathan. *The Dam Busters*. Sutton, 2005.

Middlebrook, Martin. *The Berlin Raids*. Cassell, 2000.

Middlebrook, Martin. *The Nuremberg Raid*. Pen and Sword, 2009.

THE AIRCRAFT AND CREWS

Falconer, Jonathan. *Stirling in Combat*. Sutton, 2006.

Garbett, Mike, and Goulding, Brian. *Lancaster at War 5: 50 Years On*. Ian Allan, 1995.

Merrick, K.A. *Handley Page Halifax: From Hell to Victory and Beyond*. Classic Publications, 2009.

NB: These are the most recent editions available. Some of the older titles may no longer be in print, but may still be obtainable on the second-hand market.

INDEX

Page numbers in italics refer to illustrations